GARETH GUIDES TO AN EXTRAORDINARY LIFE

Gareth's Guide to

BUILDING A ROBOT

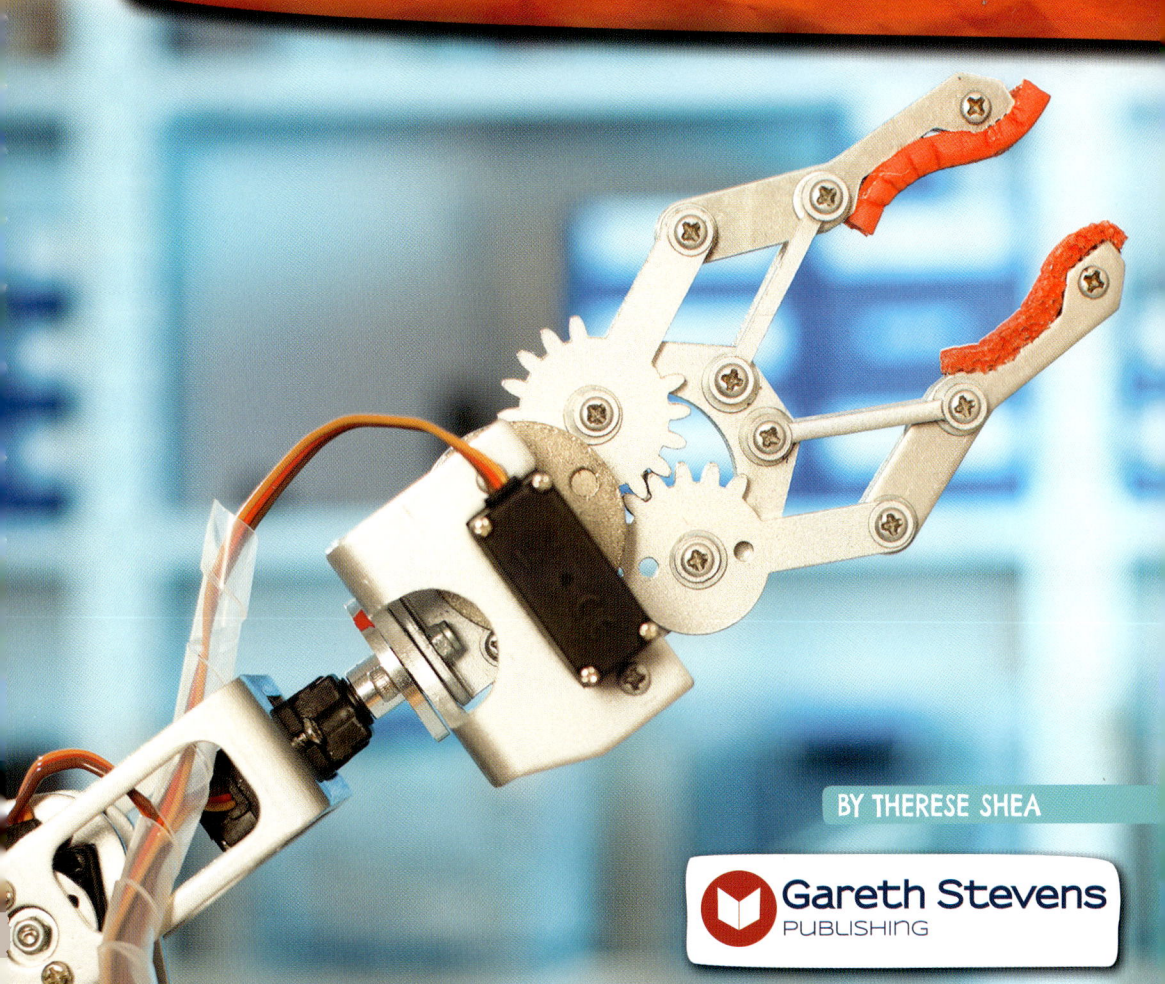

BY THERESE SHEA

Gareth Stevens
PUBLISHING

Please visit our website, www.garethstevens.com. For a free color catalog of all our high-quality books, call toll free 1-800-542-2595 or fax 1-877-542-2596.

Library of Congress Cataloging-in-Publication Data

Names: Shea, Therese, author.
Title: Gareth's guide to building a robot / Therese Shea.
Description: New York : Gareth Stevens Publishing, [2019] | Series: Gareth guides to an extraordinary life | Includes bibliographical references and index.
Identifiers: LCCN 2017050272| ISBN 9781538220511 (library bound) | ISBN 9781538220535 (pbk.) | ISBN 9781538220542 (6 pack)
Subjects: LCSH: Robots–Juvenile literature.
Classification: LCC TJ211.2 .S5358 2019 | DDC 629.8/92–dc23
LC record available at https://lccn.loc.gov/2017050272

First Edition

Published in 2019 by
Gareth Stevens Publishing
111 East 14th Street, Suite 349
New York, NY 10003

Copyright © 2019 Gareth Stevens Publishing

Editor: Therese Shea

Photo credits: Cover, pp. 1, 19 science photo/Shutterstock.com; cover, pp. 1–32 (background texture) Thiti Saichua/Shutterstock.com; cover, pp. 1–32 (design elements) VDOVINA ELENA/Shutterstock.com; p. 5 (inset) Imagno/Hulton Archive/Getty Images; p. 5 (main) Hero Images/Getty Images; p. 6 ZAM811/Shutterstock.com; p. 7 VCG/VCG via Getty Images; p. 8 NASA/JPL-Caltech; p. 9 daphnusia/Shutterstock.com; p. 11 BRENDAN SMIALOWSKI/AFP/Getty Images; p. 13 JUNG YEON-JE/AFP/Getty Images; p. 14 Achim Raschka/Wikipedia.org; pp. 15, 25 Chip Somodevilla/Getty Images; p. 16 Kittapasp/Shutterstock.com; p. 17 Thierry Falise/LightRocket via Getty Images; p. 21 ROB LEVER/AFP/Getty Images; p. 23 JHU Sheridan Libraries/Gado/Getty Images; p. 27 Brendon Thorne/Getty Images for LEGO Education/FIRST; p. 29 Science Picture Co/Getty Images.

All rights reserved. No part of this book may be reproduced in any form without permission in writing from the publisher, except by a reviewer.

Printed in the United States of America

CPSIA compliance information: Batch #CS18GS: For further information contact Gareth Stevens, New York, New York at 1-800-542-2595.

CONTENTS

Robots All Around 4
Where to Find Robots 6
Who Builds Robots? 10
The Essentials 12
Robot Dissection 14
Create and Construct 18
Artificial Intelligence 20
Asimov's Robot Rules 22
Launch Your Career 24
Robotics Clubs 26
Robots of the Future 28
Glossary 30
For More Information 31
Index 32

➡ WORDS IN THE GLOSSARY APPEAR IN **BOLD** TYPE THE FIRST TIME THEY ARE USED IN THE TEXT.

ROBOTS ALL AROUND

Did you know the word "robot" didn't exist until the 1900s? Yet today, robots are a major part of our lives, whether we live or work with a robot or enjoy products made by robots in factories. Most of these robots don't look like the humanlike machines we read about in science fiction stories. In fact, many definitions of the word "robot" emphasize not a robot's appearance, but that it performs jobs that people normally would do. Most robots can only perform a limited number of tasks, though.

You might think building a robot is unachievable for you right now. That's not true. In this book, you'll learn about all kinds of robots and find out what you can do to become the ultimate robotics engineer!

> **SPOTLIGHT!**
> THE WORD "ROBOT" ISN'T TOO OLD, BUT THE IDEA OF MAN-MADE, HUMANLIKE MACHINES HAS EXISTED FOR HUNDREDS OF YEARS!

Robots on Stage

The word "robot" was first used in English in 1923, but Czech author Karel Čapek invented the word for his 1921 play *R.U.R.* (which stands for "Rossum's Universal Robots"). He based the term on the Czech word for "forced labor." In Čapek's work, man-made figures used as slaves rise up against humans and kill them. Many fictional works since then have covered this same theme. People worry robots will develop enough intelligence to hurt them.

A robot's form often depends on the tasks it's built to do. Some robots need wheels, others look like an arm, and still others have a humanlike appearance.

WHERE TO FIND ROBOTS

Robots might seem like toys or luxuries, but they actually serve useful and serious purposes. Most robots are placed in factories to perform precise tasks that can be difficult or tiring for people to do. Robots can do these tasks again and again without stopping to rest. This means more and often better products can be manufactured.

Robots are also used by the military. They're sent in to handle dangerous tasks, such as bomb disposal. They can be **programmed** to enter buildings to find enemies and send video back. Sometimes, they're even used as spies. The military is also developing drones, or unmanned aerial vehicles, that are **autonomous**. These flying robots are programmed to act based on situations they may encounter in performing their missions.

> **SPOTLIGHT!**
> ROBOTS CAN BE TASKED WITH CLEANING UP HARMFUL CHEMICALS THAT PEOPLE SHOULDN'T BE EXPOSED TO.

drone

Robot Police Worldwide

Robots are used in law enforcement. The police department of Cleveland, Ohio, uses a 12-inch (30 cm) robot called Griffin to search for bombs in places where police can't easily fit, such as under cars. Brazilian police used robots called PackBots to look for bombs during the 2016 Summer Olympics. South Korea uses robots with cameras as prison guards. And China, Japan, and the Democratic Republic of Congo use robots to direct traffic!

6 MILES (9.7 KM) PER HOUR → speed of Brazil's PackBots

This traffic robot in China helps keep pedestrians, or people who are walking, safe!

7

Robots are found in some hospitals. They're used to show patients and visitors around. They can collect data and deliver medicines. They can help perform surgeries that require great precision, too. Doctors even use them to examine patients remotely from another location.

NASA (National Aeronautics and Space Administration) uses many kinds of robots, too. Some of the most complicated ones are exploring the planet Mars. A rover is an exploration vehicle designed to move across the surface of a planet or other space body. The rover *Curiosity*, which landed in 2012, has been acting as a geology lab on Mars. It receives orders from Earth, but also can act autonomously, such as choosing the best path to avoid obstacles.

> **➡ SPOTLIGHT!**
> NASA ROVER DRIVER JULIE TOWNSEND EXPLAINED YOU DON'T HAVE TO BE AN EXPERT TO WORK WITH ROBOTS: "IF YOU DON'T KNOW HOW TO DO SOMETHING, THAT DOESN'T MEAN YOU CAN'T DO IT—YOU JUST HAVE TO DO SOME LEARNING FIRST."

Curiosity

More Helping Robots

Robots are being tested as companions for people who have no one else to be with them. They could call for help when needed or remind the people they care for to take medicine. One robot developed by the Massachusetts Institute of Technology looks like a teddy bear. It comforts sick children and sends their **vital signs** to doctors. Other kinds of robots act as home security systems or even as alarm clocks!

120 number of US hospitals using TUG robots to transport goods and supplies to patients

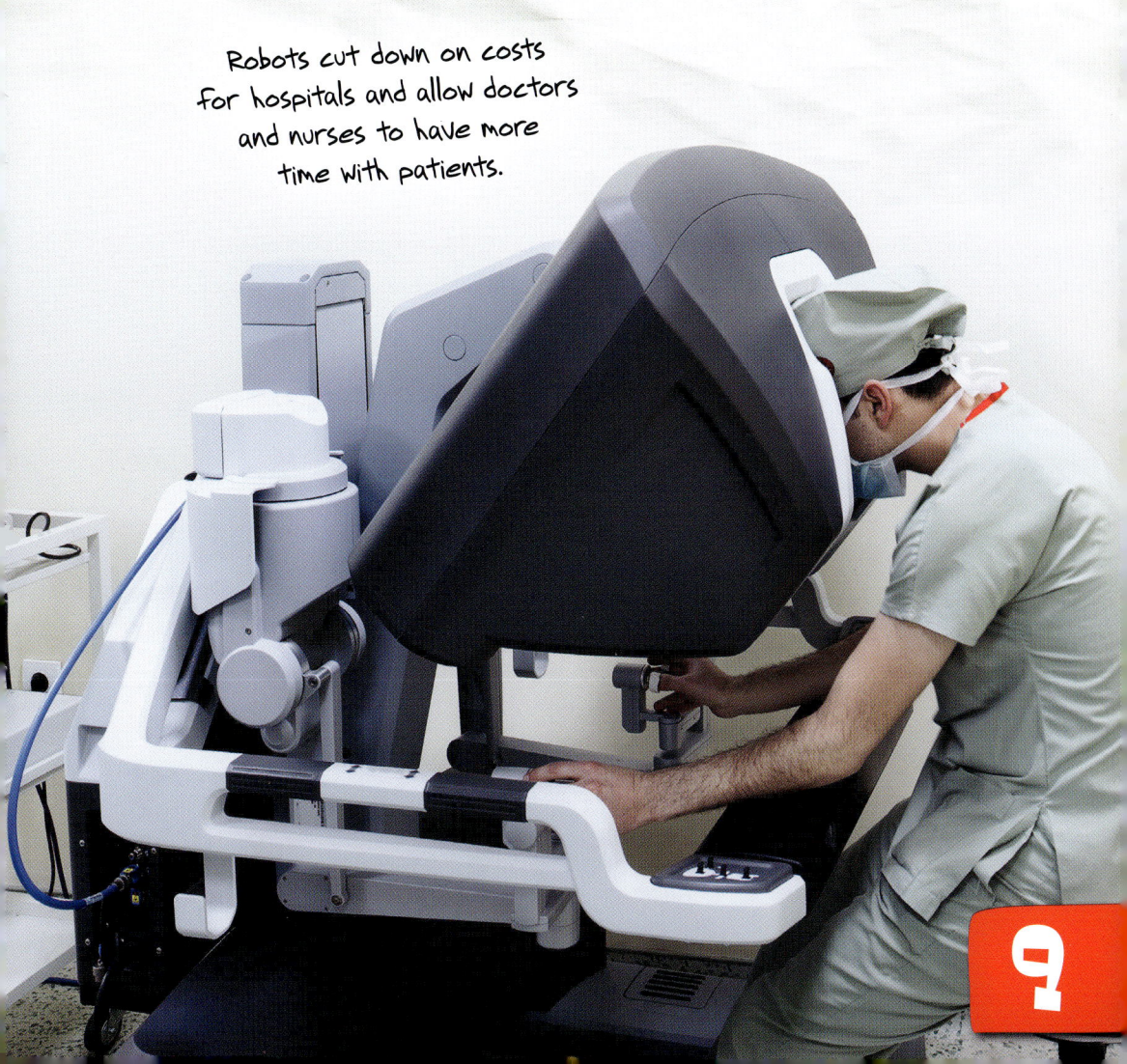

Robots cut down on costs for hospitals and allow doctors and nurses to have more time with patients.

WHO BUILDS ROBOTS?

People who build robots for a living are called robotics engineers, or roboticists. They usually have a background in many fields, including mechanical engineering, electrical engineering, and computer science.

Depending on the **complexity** of the robots, some roboticists only work on a few robots their entire career. Much of their time is split between planning and designing in an office and building and testing in a lab. Both are equally important in making sure the robot succeeds in its missions.

Roboticists are employed by industries, such as those that make cars, food products, **appliances**, and electronics. Others work in robotics labs connected with schools and the military. Still others are NASA employees, developing robots for space exploration and experiments.

142,400 → projected number of roboticist jobs in the US in 2024

> **➡ SPOTLIGHT!**
> SOME PEOPLE ARGUE THAT ROBOTS THAT ARE WHOLLY CONTROLLED REMOTELY AREN'T REALLY ROBOTS, JUST MACHINES. OTHERS DISAGREE. WHAT DO YOU THINK?

CLASSIFYING ROBOTS

PREPROGRAMMED
↳ programmed ahead of time to work in an unchanging environment. They cannot change actions. Examples are robots that work in factories.

AUTONOMOUS
↳ adapt to a changing environment without reprogramming. Examples are robot vacuums.

TELEOPERATED
↳ controlled remotely, allowing people to have contact with faraway locations. Examples are robotic arms in space.

AUGMENTING
↳ connected to a person's body, enhancing actions or allowing for actions that would otherwise be impossible. Examples are robotic limbs.

After this man lost his arm to cancer, he was fitted for a robotic arm.

11

THE ESSENTIALS

Does a career in robotics sound fascinating to you? These are some important traits that most roboticists share:

- Roboticists know how to apply math and science to real-life situations.
- Roboticists are interested in learning programming languages.
- Roboticists are curious about both designing and repairing machines.
- Roboticists are able to analyze a problem and use critical-thinking skills to identify strengths and weaknesses in solutions.
- Roboticists understand a number of systems (such as mechanics, electronics, and computer programming) and how they work together.
- Roboticists persist in finding answers to difficult problems.
- Roboticists can work and communicate with a team.

Do you share these qualities with the most talented robotics engineers? If so, you'll have no trouble fitting in at any robotics lab!

> **SPOTLIGHT!**
> ROBOTICISTS ARE USING **CLOUD COMPUTING** MORE OFTEN TO PROGRAM THEIR CREATIONS. THE CLOUD ALSO ALLOWS ROBOTICISTS TO SHARE INFORMATION WITH EACH OTHER AND OTHER ROBOTS.

Learn a Language

What programming language should you learn to program a robot? BASIC is a language designed for beginner programmers. Python is thought to be an easier language as well. Many think C and C++ are a great place for new roboticists to start because you can use them to interact with a majority of robotics hardware. The LEGO company created a visual programming language to use with their robotics kits. Programmers place pictures called icons in a certain order to make their robots act.

MORE THAN 2,000

number of programming languages in all

Perhaps the most important trait of a roboticist is creativity. Robotics calls for imagination in both designing and problem solving.

ROBOT DISSECTION

Building robots isn't only for roboticists. Many people build robots as a hobby. Like any machine, there are some basic components, or parts, that can't be left out when you're making a robot. If just one of these is missing, you might construct something that looks like a robot, but doesn't function like one.

1. computer—A robot has one or more computers. In smaller robots, the computer is often in the form of a microcontroller. This is a device that can execute a program and is usually responsible for calculations and communications.

2. power supply—Most robots are battery powered, though they might plug into an electrical outlet to power up rechargeable batteries.

SPOTLIGHT!
A ROBOT'S MICROCONTROLLER ACTS AS THE MACHINE'S "BRAIN," STORING PROGRAMS, RECEIVING INFORMATION, AND SENDING INSTRUCTIONS THROUGH AN ELECTRICAL CIRCUIT.

microcontroller

Safety First!

Even if you're building a hobby robot, you need to think about safety. It's a good idea to review your plans with an adult. If your plans include power tools such as drills, an adult should be present. You may also need to wear safety glasses and gloves while working with certain tools. Anytime you work with electricity, you should ask an adult to oversee your work. A badly wired robot could shock you and ruin expensive parts.

Which States Use the Most Industrial Robots? [2015]

- MICHIGAN → 28,000
- OHIO → 20,400
- INDIANA → 19,400

This robot was programmed to plug itself in when its battery needs to be charged!

3. moving parts—Some robots just look like wheels, while others have many more movable parts. Parts may be connected with joints, much like the bones of the human body.

4. actuators— The actuators convert (usually electrical) energy into motion. They act as a robot's muscles. The microcontroller signals the actuators to create motion in the robot's parts through an electrical circuit.

5. sensors—Some robots have the ability to react to their environment. They use sensors to collect information such as movement, temperature, touch, sound, and light. Sensors may be video cameras or temperature **gauges**.

You may also choose to place lights, speakers, screens that display words, and other **accessories** on your robot. The maker chooses how complex their creation will be.

> **SPOTLIGHT!**
> MANY ROBOTS REQUIRE MOTOR CONTROLLERS. THESE ARE ELECTRONIC DEVICES THAT PROVIDE THE ELECTRICAL CURRENT NEEDED TO DRIVE THE ACTUATORS SINCE THE MICROCONTROLLER HAS LIMITED POWER.

servo motor

Making Motion

Actuators are devices that convert power to movement. Industrial robots are often driven by either a hydraulic system, which uses pressurized liquid, or a pneumatic system, which uses pressurized gas, because of the high speed and force these systems create. Other robots use electric motors and **solenoids** as actuators. Servos are electric motors that rotate or push parts of a machine. Hobby servos come in many shapes and sizes.

This humanlike robot, named ChihiraAico, is able to move with the help of 43 pneumatic actuators in its shoulders, arms, hands, and face.

CREATE AND CONSTRUCT

After you collect the parts of your robot, you'll have to put them together correctly. First, decide on a design and make a frame to act as the robot's body. Use new materials or reuse something you already have, such as a plastic container. Measure your parts to make sure everything fits according to your design. Use glue, screws, nails, or even tape to place everything in or on the frame.

Still, the robot won't work until the right parts are connected. For example, the microcontroller must be connected to one or more batteries to give it power, and all sensors must be connected to the microcontroller to provide it with data about the environment. The actuators are joined to wheels, tracks, arms, and other moving parts.

> **SPOTLIGHT!**
> ROBOTICS KITS PROVIDE ALL ROBOT PARTS AS WELL AS INSTRUCTIONS FOR HOW TO PUT THEM TOGETHER AND PROGRAM THE ROBOT.

Deciding on a Design

You want your robot to look good, but you also want it to accomplish something. When determining your robot's design, also keep in mind its purpose. Address these questions: How will it move? How will it know about its environment? Will it move things in its environment? If so, how? **Integrate** the answers to these questions into your design along with the robot's other basic parts and accessories.

Building a robot can get expensive depending on what parts are used and the complexity of the design. Save money by shopping around for parts or using items you already have on hand.

ARTIFICIAL INTELLIGENCE

You can build a robot and program it. But will it be "intelligent"? You've probably heard the term "artificial intelligence," or AI. This means different things to different roboticists. Many think it means the ability of computers (such as those in robots) to solve problems, reason, and learn from past experiences, just like people can. While some robots can do these things in a limited way, no computer has been programmed to achieve the level of intelligence of a human being yet.

However, some robots can mimic, or copy, people's actions. They may be able to store successful actions in their memory to repeat them in the future in similar situations. This is a step toward artificial intelligence.

> **SPOTLIGHT!**
> A ROBOT IN HUMAN FORM IS CALLED AN ANDROID. MANY AI ROBOTICISTS CONSTRUCT ANDROIDS BECAUSE IT'S EASIER FOR PEOPLE TO INTERACT WITH HUMANLIKE ROBOTS.

The Turing Test

British computer scientist Alan Turing created a test in 1950 to determine if a computer was truly intelligent: A computer and a person are asked identical questions. If the computer is truly intelligent, the questioner will be unable to tell the machine's answers from the person's. In 1991, a man named Hugh Loebner created the Loebner Prize, promising $100,000 to the first person to build a computer that passes the Turing test. No computer—or robot—has passed it yet.

Some robots can be programmed to play chess, but that doesn't mean they're intelligent. Instead, they've been programmed with the rules of the game and are able to analyze the outcome of every move!

Asimov's Robot Rules

As robots have become more intelligent and become key tools of law enforcement and the military, **debate** has arisen about whether they should ever be programmed to harm others. Isaac Asimov, a famous science fiction writer, invented some guidelines to govern a robot's purpose. In a short story published in 1942, he wrote the "Three Rules of Robotics":

1. A robot may not injure a human being or, through inaction, allow a human being to come to harm.

2. A robot must obey orders given to it by human beings except where such orders would conflict with the First Law.

3. A robot must protect its own existence as long as such protection does not conflict with the First or Second Law.

Many roboticists quote these and believe they should be followed when creating a robot's mission.

SPOTLIGHT!

IN 2015, EXPERTS IN THE FIELDS OF ARTIFICIAL INTELLIGENCE—INCLUDING BUSINESSMAN ELON MUSK AND SCIENTIST STEPHEN HAWKING—SIGNED A LETTER ENCOURAGING A BAN ON ROBOTS PROGRAMMED TO KILL.

I, Robot

Isaac Asimov (1920-1992) was an author as well as a biochemist. He wrote around 500 books and explained science concepts in his works so that people who weren't scientists could understand them. In his short-story collection *I, Robot* (1950), he developed a set of **ethics** for robots that influenced how other authors wrote about robots. And as robots became actual machines in the real world, scientists looked to his ideas, too.

Isaac Asimov was the first to use the word "robotics."

LAUNCH YOUR CAREER

You can start preparing for your career in robotics today. Pay attention to your classes in school. You'll build on that knowledge in high school and college. Math and physics are especially important in engineering. Physics is the science of energy and mechanics, which are both important in successfully building and operating a robot. Since your robot will have a computer and need to be programmed to perform tasks, computer science is also a valuable subject.

Some colleges offer degrees in robotics, but it's more common for students to get a good educational foundation in college and then pursue a higher degree in robotics in graduate school. Many schools have special robotics laboratories that are excellent environments for students to build and research.

> **SPOTLIGHT!**
> WORCESTER POLYTECHNIC INSTITUTE IN WORCESTER, MASSACHUSETTS, WAS THE FIRST COLLEGE TO OFFER A ROBOTICS UNDERGRADUATE DEGREE, BEGINNING IN 2007.

Robotics = Three in One

Would you want to work on a robot's brain, muscles, or nervous system? Roboticists in training may wish to focus on one of three areas in robotics. They may concentrate on mechanical engineering to work on the design of the robot and how it moves. They may choose to focus on electrical engineering to work on its electrical circuits. Or, they may be most interested in working on the robot's brain and focus on computer science.

Six Top US Robotics Engineering Schools

> Carnegie Mellon University (Pittsburgh, PA)
> University of Michigan (Ann Arbor, MI)
> Georgia Institute of Technology (Atlanta, GA)
> Oregon State University (Corvallis, OR)
> Johns Hopkins University (Baltimore, MD)
> Massachusetts Institute of Technology (Cambridge, MA)

Roboticists from Carnegie Mellon and Worcester Polytechnic teamed up to create this robot meant to aid people after natural or man-made disasters.

ROBOTICS CLUBS

While the most complex robots are built by engineers with years of education and training, you might be surprised to learn that many robots are built by elementary and high school students! In fact, most roboticists highly recommend working on robots outside of school in order to gain experience for careers later in life.

There are robotics kits, such as LEGO Mindstorms, that take you step-by-step through building a robot by yourself. Many libraries and schools have robotics clubs that give you hands-on practice with design, programming, electronics, and more. You can work with a team to build a robot or work on your own. Clubs are often led by experienced people who can guide you and answer questions you may have.

> ### SPOTLIGHT!
> NASA AEROSPACE ENGINEER LYNDON BRIDGWATER BELIEVES, "THE SKILLS NEEDED TO DESIGN, BUILD, AND WORK IN A MULTIDISCIPLINE TEAM AND CHANGE THE WORLD [THROUGH ROBOTICS] ONLY COME THROUGH EXPERIENCE. PROJECT-BASED CLASSES OR ROBOTICS COMPETITIONS ARE BY FAR THE BEST WAY TO GAIN THESE SKILLS."

Robotics FIRST

Some of the most famous robotics competitions are organized by an organization called FIRST (For Inspiration and Recognition of Science and Technology). Students as young as 6 as well as teenagers participate. These exciting events are meant to spark interest in technology, inspiring young people to become leaders in science-related fields. More than $50 million in scholarships have been awarded to participants since 1989. FIRST participants are more likely to go on to major in science or engineering degrees in college.

MORE THAN 460,000

estimated number of students in FIRST robotics competitions (2016-2017)

FIRST robotics teams have up to 10 students. You don't need any experience with robotics to join—you'll learn quickly!

ROBOTS OF THE FUTURE

People often worry that robots will take over their jobs someday. While robots may replace people in performing some tasks, there will always be a need for people to construct, program, repair, and oversee robots.

The uses for robots are only limited by our needs and our imaginations. Robots may be the key to the future of space exploration. They could be used to travel to locations too distant or dangerous for human astronauts. They may have an essential role in medicine, too. Tiny robots called nanorobots may one day be able to enter the human body to perform surgery and **administer** medicine. Robots could also be programmed to build more of themselves and other objects, too. Will you engineer robots like these someday?

$95,000 → average annual salary of a roboticist

> **SPOTLIGHT!**
>
> SHAWN DOUGLAS, A RESEARCHER AT THE UNIVERSITY OF CALIFORNIA IN SAN FRANCISCO, SAYS HE LOOKED TO NATURE WHEN DESIGNING NANOBOTS IN MEDICINE: "WE'RE USING THE SAME MATERIALS THAT CELLS USE TO REALLY GREAT EFFECT, WE'RE REPURPOSING THOSE FOR MEDICINE."

Future Numbers

According to research firm International Data Corporation, the growth of robotics in the years to come will create many job opportunities. The firm suggests that not enough people are training for a career in robotics today and forecasts that about 35 percent of robotics-related jobs will be unfilled by 2020. The researchers further predict the average salary in robotics will increase by 60 percent. So, careers in robotics will be more plentiful and more profitable.

This image illustrates how nanorobots (colored blue) might look circulating in the bloodstream.

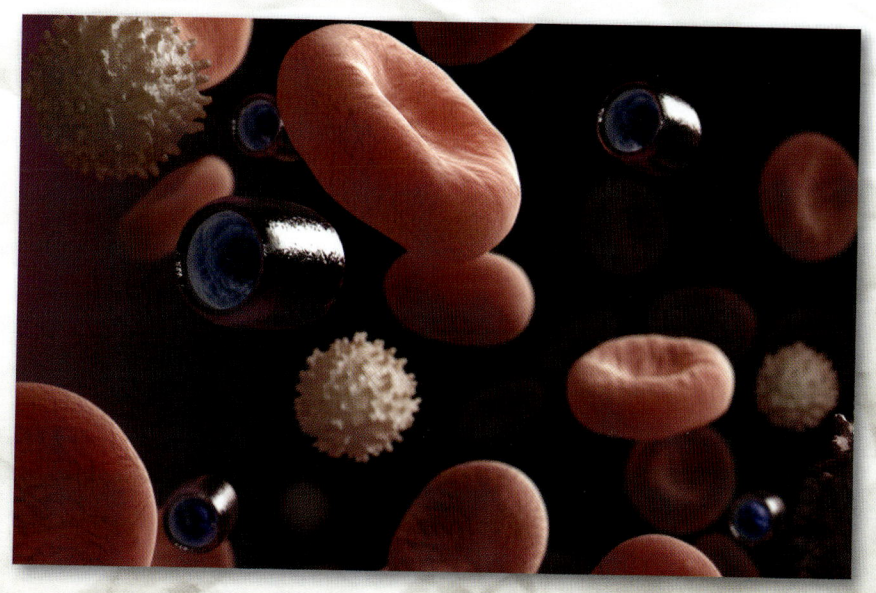

Tips for Becoming a Top Roboticist

> Study math, physics, computer science, and related subjects.

> Join a robotics club.

> Build robots as a hobby.

> Enter competitions with a robot you or your club has built.

> Attend college and graduate school focusing on robotics, mechanical engineering, electrical engineering, or computer science.

> Decide whether to work for a research lab, private industry, the military, or NASA.

> Continue to learn about breakthroughs in the robotics industry while excelling in your career!

GLOSSARY

accessory: something added to something else to make it more useful or effective

administer: to give a drug or medicine to someone

appliance: a machine that is powered by electricity and that is used in people's houses to perform a particular job

autonomous: acting separately from people

cloud computing: the practice of storing regularly used computer data on multiple servers that can be accessed through the internet

complexity: the state of having many parts that can be difficult to understand

debate: a discussion between people in which they express different opinions about something

ethics: rules of behavior based on ideas about what is morally good and bad

gauge: an instrument that is used for measuring something

integrate: to make something a part of another larger thing

program: to give a computer a set of instructions to perform a particular action

solenoid: a coil of wire that when carrying a current acts like a magnet and that is used especially as a switch or control for a mechanical device

vital signs: important body functions such as breathing and heartbeat that are measured to see if someone is alive or healthy

For More Information

Books

La Bella, Laura. *The Future of Robotics*. New York, NY: Rosen Publishing, 2018.

Larson, Kirsten W. *Hobby Robots*. Mankato, MN: Amicus, 2018.

Sobey, Edwin J. C. *Robotics Engineering: Learn It, Try It!* North Mankato, MN: Capstone Press, 2018.

Websites

How Robots Work
science.howstuffworks.com/robot.htm
Check out this article before attempting your first hobby robot.

Robotics Career Profiles
www.nasa.gov/audience/foreducators/robotics/careercorner/
Read advice from these NASA robotics engineers.

Publisher's note to educators and parents: Our editors have carefully reviewed these websites to ensure that they are suitable for students. Many websites change frequently, however, and we cannot guarantee that a site's future contents will continue to meet our high standards of quality and educational value. Be advised that students should be closely supervised whenever they access the internet.

INDEX

androids 20
artificial intelligence (AI) 20, 21, 22
Asimov, Isaac 22, 23
autonomy 6, 8, 11
basic components 14, 16, 17, 18, 19
Čapek, Karel 5
cloud computing 12
clubs 26, 29
competitions 26, 27, 29
Curiosity 8
drones 6
education 13, 24, 25, 26, 27, 29
essential traits 12, 13
factories 4, 6, 11
hobby robots 14, 15, 17, 29
hospitals 8, 9
humanlike robots 4, 5, 17, 20
I, Robot 23
intelligence 5, 20, 21, 22

law enforcement 7, 22
Loebner Prize 21
medicine 8, 9, 28
military, the 6, 10, 22, 29
nanorobots 28, 29
NASA 8, 10, 26, 29
programming 6, 11, 12, 15, 18, 20, 21, 22, 24, 26, 28
programming languages 12, 13
R.U.R. (*Rossum's Universal Robots*) 5
robotic limbs 11
robotics kits 13, 18, 26
safety 15
salary 28, 29
"Three Rules of Robotics" 22
Turing test 21
Turing, Alan 21
types of robots 11